How to Start a Consulting Business from Scratch

How I Became a Consultant in Just 3 Months

By

Jim Busby

Les Forman

CSB Academy Publishing Co.
P. O. Box 966
Semmes, Alabama 36575, USA

Cover Design
By
Angela Anderson
First Edition

Contents

Our Story

In case you wonder if you have what it takes to be a consultant, without knowing you, I would say you may have it in you. But if you have doubt, then maybe it is time to do some self-evaluation and realization and see if you really have it in you. Read on, and I will tell you what you need to find within yourself to know if you can do this job or not.

I co-authored this book with Jim because I was motivated and inspired by him; he showed me that everyone has something in them that can help others. The very first day we met, he told me, "As long as you know little more than the next guy, you are an Expert on that topic." Later he told me it was Tim Ferris who said that originally. I never thought I had any skills to be a consultant, but he did convince me otherwise and took me under his wing, taught me everything I know, and here I am.

Okay a little bit about us first. I am Les Forman, I have an associate degree in Marketing, but that was a long time ago. Until I met Jim, I was working for a local newspaper in the advertising/Classified Dept. As newspapers are dying out everywhere in this country, I knew I would lose my job eventually, but wasn't sure how soon or how fast. Then one day I met Jim Busby who has been a well-known consultant in the marketing field. He was hired by our newspaper to see if he could save the day by creating some innovative marketing ideas that would boost subscription thus sales and make our paper survive longer.

Long story short, I worked with (well mostly watched him) him for three months. He did do some wonders for our paper, which saved it from closing its doors. But when he was leaving, he asked me if I would be interested in working with him. I wanted to learn; I was fascinated by his work, his personality so I said YES.

Next thing I knew, I left my newspaper job and joined forces with him. He needed me to take his "Spillover" work; he was busy doing bigger consulting projects, so there were mini-consulting jobs that he didn't have time for, so he gave them to me and coached me to do them.

I started making 3x more money than what I was making in my newspaper job, not to mention I started traveling all over the country and in just five months I build up enough confidence that I figured out I could do it on my own and without his help. No, I didn't leave his company, but I became more independent where I didn't ask his help often.

One year after I joined him, he told me I was ready, and I should get started on my own and that he was thinking about retiring.

Anyway, that is another story. I didn't let him retire, he is still active, but now I do most of the legwork, and I let him relax a little. But he did tell me we should write a book together and share and teach people how to become consultants. Now, neither of us are good in writing; we are only good in marketing consulting, but we decided to give it a try. So here we are...

Before you read the book, have an open mind, do not doubt yourself in advance, remember the very first thing you need in this field is CONFIDENCE, then you need some expertise on the subject. But Confidence is what can make or break you.

Jim told me early on that there are only two reasons most companies hire consultants nowadays. Either it is to improve some parts of their company, or to play a blame shifting game if things go wrong. See, no top-level management wants to be "under the radar" they don't want to admit it was their decision if something were to go wrong. But if something happens to go right, they can always take the reward. By hiring a consultant, they can have it both ways.

He also said, "If you know little more than the next guy on a subject, then you inject confidence into that mix you are a winner, provided you are willing to learn more and motivate yourself to learn and adapt to any situation. But be prepared to take the fall if things don't go right."

Looking back at my own life, I never thought I could be a marketing consultant. I don't have the education nor do I have the skills for it. But he taught me it is not the education that makes you a great consultant. If that were the case, then every Ph.D. in marketing would take our job. It is the mix of confidence, knowledge, willingness to learn and adapt are what makes someone a great and successful consultant.

I am the living proof of that. Before we take any new contract, I study the company that is hiring us; I brainstorm new marketing ideas, I talk to average everyday people and ask random questions to figure out how they view the company or the product, for that matter. So in a way, I get started before I start. Make sense?

Here is the one more example. My wife has been in the makeup business for many years. She works for a national brand makeup company part-time. I knew she knows about women's makeup more than average women do, so I told her to become a beauty consultant. She replied that she was happy in what she is doing, and she didn't think she had the knowledge or the 'know how' to be a consultant. I did some legwork on her behalf and landed her the very first $3,500 consulting job for a local pageant show. She was scared but excited at the same time. After finishing her first gig, she quit her job, and now she has her successful beauty consulting business where is she made little over $87,000 last year, but she only worked seven months out of the year.

Now I have to share this last one before we start. My nephew didn't finish college, despite all the effort and money my brother spent trying to put him through college. He took a job at one of the office supply places making photocopies.

One thing I knew about him is that he knew how to use Facebook and Twitter and all those social media. When I was getting started, I called him to help me set up my own Facebook and other social media pages. I am sure most of you know someone who is good at that sort of things.

In one of my consulting jobs, one day they asked me if I could recommend someone for social media consulting as they needed some help with their social media presence. Without thinking I recommended my nephew, and he got the job! Long story short, he is on his 3rd contract, and he too left his office supply job.

Okay, hope I was able to make a point that you do not need a Ph.D. or a master's degree to be a successful consultant. But please read through this book's material then take a piece of a paper and write down what you think you are good at, what are your strengths, and what your weaknesses are.

Then pick the one you think you are most comfortable with and start working towards it. It will not happen overnight, but if you can follow the marketing tips and market yourself right, you should see some degree of success in about six months.

What is Consulting Business?

Every field of business has its experts. Those are the ones that managed to find out what works and what doesn't and how to maintain a heightened level of competitiveness in the fields of work in which they operate. Speaking in business terms, an expert is defined as a professional who has acquired knowledge and skills through study and practice over the years, in a particular field or subject, to the extent that his or her opinion may be helpful in fact-finding, problem-solving, or understanding of a situation.[1]

As an expert, one has the opportunity to choose from two possible career paths. One of the paths an expert can choose is pretty obvious... to continue working in his or her field of expertise as a very performant individual. The second career path an expert can choose to follow is to become a consultant.

The dictionary defines the consultant as a person who provides expert advice in a professional matter. By becoming a consultant, the expert chooses to share his experience and knowledge with others who are interested in becoming experts themselves. By doing so, the consultant engages in a mission to help others reach their potential and become better at what they do in their areas of expertise.

Consulting is considered to be one of the noblest professions in the world because the sole foundation on which it is built is based on helping others. Just like a doctor cures and helps a patient live a more fulfilling life, a consultant helps his "patients" to become better at what they do and to overcome the obstacles they face while getting there.

---

[1] http://www.businessdictionary.com/definition/expert.html

The consulting industry has its point of origin in the US when, in the late 1950s, consultants had started to appear in all branches of the business world. Before this time, consultants were found only in fields like finance, employment and legal. But in the 1960s, when the US economy shifted from being production oriented to being service oriented. This new shift proved to be the perfect catalyst for a novel wide-spread consulting industry. Because they positioned themselves as experts in their fields, the companies who were seeking their expertise managed to generate great demand for their field of work. This trend continued and had been refined over the years. Today, companies around the world seek the expertise of consultants for ten main reasons:

1. Companies want to benefit from their particular expertise and know-how, that they believe their own employees lack. In this case, a successful record of satisfied clients speaks wonders in getting new ones from recommendations.

2. Sometimes it is very hard for a manager to spot the problems inside his organization. This is why they hire consultants to bring in what is called the fresh eye effect and the necessary perspective needed to spot the problems the organization struggles with.

3. Sometimes companies find out that is more cost effective to hire consultants when wanting to supplement their staff instead of hiring full-time employees. This way companies can save thousands of dollars and benefit from the increased experience and know-how only a consultant can bring to the table.

Even if, at first, hiring a full-time employee may seem the obvious, more cost-efficient approach, in the long run, the consultant option tends to be the most reasonable option.

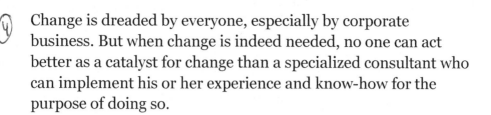

Change is dreaded by everyone, especially by corporate business. But when change is indeed needed, no one can act better as a catalyst for change than a specialized consultant who can implement his or her experience and know-how for the purpose of doing so.

Companies hire consultants also for their objective outlook on things. Problems and issues can be difficult to spot for the internal staff because they've developed in the same environment. This is why a keen expert viewpoint over the current situation they are facing is enough to identify and isolate the problem or issue that is keeping the company performing poorly. As an added bonus, the consultant can also offer the solution to the identified problem or issue since his or her areas of expertise focus exactly on the area the problem originated from.

They hire a consultant for their knowledge and special skills that they can teach to the employees in the pursuance of making them perform better, have better results or optimize areas of their work that can be improved. Because of this, consultants must always stay at the top of their fields and up-to-date on all developments and latest advancements in their fields of work, so nothing but the latest and most accurate information can be passed onto the employees that need improving in their lines of work.

Sometimes a company has to take unpleasant actions like program or personnel cuts. For those types of actions to be as neutral as possible, companies hire consultants to do those "dirty jobs" for them. Besides that, a consultant might know the best possible approaches to limit "bad blood" on both sides.

All companies go through the same life cycle: the coming into existence, the period of growth, stagnation and then collapse. The only period of time in the life of a company, a manager or a shareholder wants to be in is the growth period. But for a company to remain in the growth period for a longer period of time, it must remain competitive on the market.

 A company is competitive only when competitive ideas are put into place. Sometimes those ideas come from the hired personnel itself. Sometimes it comes from hired consultants that specialize themselves in bringing new life into companies that have reached the stagnation period of their lifecycle.

To prevent the imminent collapse of the company, consultants are hired to identify the problems that have led the company to this current state and generate solutions that will rescue it and put it on the right track once again.

 Another period in the life of a company when a consultant is highly sought after is the initial coming into being. Many entrepreneurs seek guidance from business development consultants that have specialized themselves in building companies based on groundbreaking ideas.

There are hundreds of people out there, maybe thousands, with novel business ideas who need guidance on how to put their ideas into place in the most efficient way possible. This is where the business development consultants come into place, to offer their support.

Every business owner knows that the most important aspect that can determine a company to prosper of to go bankrupt, its clients. More clients mean more profit and sharper growth, while little to none means a lazy advance or even death.

Some business consultants specialize on how to better attract customers or possess large contacts databases that a business owner can use to attract new prospects. These types of consultants are dearly sought after because of their ability to generate a steady influx of new business, which every company desires.

Those are just a handful of the reasons why companies hire consultants. Since the shift of the economy has gone from focusing on production to focusing on services in the early 1960s the need for consultants has skyrocketed and never stopped since.

As a consultant, you can come from a wide array of domains like:

Accounting. All businesses need bookkeeping and tax preparation, regardless of their size. This makes accounting a solid career path for any expert accountant, who is willing to help others in financial matters.

 Advertising. This domain is crucial to any business that is looking to expand their client base. Companies seek advertising consultants that can help them develop advertising campaigns.

Career. Recent corporate downsizing has left the job market with huge demand for and an insufficient number of job positions. Because of this, experts in the field of human resources and career counseling have taken the role of consultants, all in pursuance of helping the unfortunate many who are in seek of a job. They do so by helping job seekers reinvent themselves, brighten up their CVs and make themselves pop in the eyes of the employer. This shows that a career in consulting is not reserved only for the corporate part of the economy and that sometimes it can very well address individuals.

Computer/IT. IT is booming right now, so it is only fair to assume that if you have any expertise in internet related processes, software development or hardware installation, companies will be willing to pay for your counseling.

Education. Another field in which consulting can be turned into a fulfilling career is the field of education. Just like career counseling, this field has nothing to do with companies and addresses the individual. These days, with all the possibilities lurking in the world, choosing a career path while still young can be more difficult than thought possible. This is where an education consultant might come in handy to the ones that want to choose their education in accordance with their inborn abilities and talents.

Human Resources. Companies will always look for help when it comes to personnel issues, conflict resolution, violence, communication deficiency and matters that are best left to the experts.

Head Hunting. As long as it will be cheaper to externalize processes like executive search and personnel selection, companies will always ask help from outside sources like other specialized companies and consultants.

Insurance. Many consultants take great pride in helping people find the best prices for their insurance needs. This is another viable consulting career path that a specialist can take when wanting to interact with individuals rather than companies.

Management. Probably the most widespread consulting field, the management consulting field is ever in demand. Managers are always seeking new ideas on how to better run their business and transform the hard economic times they face today into opportunities. This field of consulting will always be in high demand for experienced individuals who are willing to share their ideas and know-how with others.

Public Relations. Businesses around the world benefit from qualitative press coverage. There will always be demand for public relations consultants who can put a company in the best light possible in the eyes of the press and media.

Those are just a handful of fields in which consultants can thrive. Later on, we will take the top 20 consulting business niches and explain them in greater detail. But until then we will attempt to answer a critical question everyone must ask themselves when attempting to start a career in consulting.

Why is The Demand for Consultancy Growing?

Today's businesses are progressively more focused on new technologies and novel ideas that have the potential to further their growth and bring a better profit. Because of this, there is a greater request for the right people who can assist the company to grow and strive for ever larger profit with the right ideas and know-how. The professionals, also known as consultants, are the forerunners of every field of expertise and can be found either in consulting firms or on their own.

The current economy has reached a state where every company who wishes to succeed must invest in all of its departments and production factors. With new technologies appearing at an ever increasingly overnight pace, new businesses strive to become competitive fast, while well-established, mature companies are fighting to remain in their forerunning positions.

This environment is the perfect context in which consulting businesses can thrive. The demand for valuable information and know-how is at an all-time high and continues to rise, and novel ideas and points of view are perceived as invaluable competition raising factors. Because of this current state of events, qualitative consultants in every domain are highly sought after.

One example of how the demand for consultancy has increased over the past years is the digital consultancy sector.

Now that all sectors of the business are being rapidly digitized, it is safe to say that all businesses who want to remain competitive in the current market must invest in IT and the digital sector. But for a company to successfully invest in the development of a department or field it must require assistance from professionals. Otherwise, the investment is at risk of being inefficient or perform poorly once fully implemented.

Because of this existing risk, companies who wish to invest into their digital sector (almost all companies on the market) seek the help of specialized IT consultants, who bring both experience and the required know-how needed to make the investment as cost-effective and productive as possible. With this in mind, there is no wonder that IT consultancy firms are booming right now, with a positive prospect on their horizons.

All these changes in the current state of things demand a change of approach every once in a while. The emergence of new technologies and the dynamic shifts of the market in which companies operate will ensure that there will always be demand for consultants as long as the market doesn't reach a stagnant dynamic.

Despite the economic crisis that hit the world hard back in 2008 and how the companies responded to it, and to the ever-changing market dynamics that followed since, the overall trend of the market was to increase their demand for external consulting, as a response to economic growth and emerging new opportunities. This trend is easily visible at a closer analysis of the current market as consulting companies such as Cognizant exceeded growth rates larger than 20% in 2015.

The needs for companies to adapt to the competitive market and remain competitive in the digital age remain as crucial as ever. And with ever-increasing client expectations, the need for specialized external consultants is higher than ever and continues to grow, as it did since it appeared in the late 1960s.

Another great example is the financial consultancy firms like EY, KPMG, and Deloitte, who are hiring in massive numbers due to growing consultancy demand. Just EY alone has more than 3,100 people hired in consulting fields and plans to supplement that number with another 1,000 in the year to come. And in the future, the EY consultancy department is estimated to reach 7,100 people. This trend is due to determined growth plans, stiff performance improvement and higher risk compliance that work together to make companies demand service from specialized consulting firms.

Following the same trend, firms like Bain & Co, PwC, Deloitte, and KPMG are also planning to hire massively in response to the same triggers. In all sectors of economic activity, be it infrastructure, FMCG, insurance or retail, there is a predominant excitement that makes managers from around the world invest in consulting services. KPMG, financial firms closely related to EY, PwC, and Deloitte, are also planning to reach 7,500 people, hired in consulting sectors by the end of 2017.

In India, for example, a country where the consulting business is booming like never before, the market is divided into three brackets. The strategic consultancy sectors, where big companies such as McKinsey, BCG, and Bain & Co. are helping other firms devise their overall managerial strategy. Then there is the sector where firms like the ones mentioned above and others like Grant Thornton are involved into low-ticket projects.

Finally, there is the last part of the market, where small-sized firms are offering their experience and know-how to other firms who are looking for such expertise in exchange for income. All of the consulting sectors of the Indian market are hiring specialized consultants in great numbers. But what it is truly fascinating is that this trend is not only reserved for the Indian or US market but in recent years has expanded to the entire global market.

This trend has been widely observable in all sector of economic activity in all developing and developed countries around the world.

More focused on business than ever, management consulting firms have been greatly influenced by changing trends over the last 20 years. One of those trends has been business reengineering, where businesses from around the world, in order to survive the ever-changing marking climate had to either reorient their activity or change it in such a way that was by the market's demand.

Today, as companies from around the world are ever more focused on customer satisfaction, delivering good products, building new businesses branched from the ground up and segmenting their customers in competitive new ways, there is an immense growth potential for the consulting businesses and the consulted ones alike.

Another determining trend that seems to impact the consulting business is the atomization of business. It seems that modern developed markets tend to favor the specialized small businesses in spite of the bigger more generalized ones. This leaves the modern day consultant with new opportunities for growth and development that come with never before seen indices of specialization.

Because new small businesses are popping up all over the globe, due to the better electronic tools available today that make market navigation easier and more efficient, some of the best consultants shift their focus towards working for small firms instead. Working for smaller firms brings better autonomy, greater impact and a heightened sense of importance, which the modern day consultant seems to be very keen on.

Regardless of the type of client a consultant or consulting firms seem to prefer, one thing is certain; there will always be demand for specialized individuals who have valuable information and know-how to share. This means that if you or someone else is to choose a career in consulting, as long as that person is an expert in its field that can deliver valuable information, there will always be demand for him or her on the market.

In the past, the big consulting firms had priority in the eyes of corporations and big companies who were seeking specialized help. Back then, it was pretty troublesome for a small consulting firm to enter the market and acquire big contracts just because of their downscaled size.

But today, in the current market dynamic the size of the consulting company you are representing is not a contracting criterion anymore. Today, big and small companies who are looking for external consulting seek only one thing... results. So as long as a consultant can deliver the promised results, a company, indiscriminate of its size will hire him.

This gives an immense opportunity to experts from every field of business to start their own consulting firms. Even better, it is said that the best consultants on the market work on their own, as freelancers, with great success.

But with such great demand and professional reward, there is also the risk of overpopulation on the international or local consulting markets. If you, by chance, tried to search for consulting firms on the internet in the past, you could've been star struck by the sheer immense number of consultants and consulting firms that are available for hire on today's market.

Although it can be immensely rewarding to work in the field of consulting, it is very hard to enter the market and make a name for yourself in an environment that is first looking for past successful projects and key references. For this particular reason, it is advisable by many to start a career in consulting by first getting hired by a well renowned consulting firm.

The newer you are in the consulting business, the bigger the firm that hires you should be. So you can gather the experience needed to start your own venture. But, let's face it, no big consulting firm would hire someone without any experience, right? But what if they are looking to hire someone for other jobs such as an assistant, receptionist or even someone who can run errands? You just need to get your foot in the door at first.

But there are also the exceptions. People who manage to make a name for themselves, without being associated with an existing consulting company. It is said that only one in ten last for more than ten years on their own. But those who do it, make it really big.

With that fair warning being said it is good to assume that with such a great demand coming from the market, as long as you possess the required expertise and people skills needed to share the information and know-how you possess, you have a pretty good chance to make a career out of consulting.

Knowing all this, we will now take the top 20 consulting business niches in the US and analyze them separately, in the pursuance of giving further insights regarding every one of them, in an individual matter.

Top 20 Consulting Fields For You to Consider

As promised earlier, we will take the top 20 consulting business niches in the USA and explain them, leaving you to decide which one best suits your preferences and professional background.

According to the latest statistics, here are the top twenty consulting businesses in the United States:

ACCOUNTING

One of the most popular professions, this field of work also heralds great responsibilities. As an accounting consultant, you must prepare, analyze, store and interpret the different implications of the business's financial statements. Being a high demand job with a heightened risk of error, most licensing authorities expect at least a university degree, high discipline and a valid business license from every accounting consultant want to be.

An accounting consultant is required to provide relevant and accurate advice regarding business financial matters to its clients. In this field of work, most practitioners operate on their own, and because of this, it is highly required for them to keep a close relationship with their clients. Otherwise, they might seek to employ a full-time accountant to do this kind of work for them. As an accounting consultant, you should accept responsibilities such as the proper determination of needed accounting services, financial forecasting, financial statements analysis, determining possibilities for the business to save money through analyzing the accounts payable and setting up the best accounting practices to satisfy your clients' needs in the best possible way.

ADVERTISING

The price of advertising consultancy has reached all-time highs. There is absolutely no wonder that more and more people who possess the required expertise want to make a career out of adverting consultancy.

As an advertising consultant, you take a wide assortment of responsibilities, starting from pitching new advertising campaigns to helping the contracting team realizing the client's vision and brainstorming. Advertising consultants may also work closely with the director of advertising in the pursuance of creating new clients.

As independent workers, consultants tend to build up large sums of connections and clients with which they have worked in the past. This base of clients that the advertising consultant brings to the table is hugely inexpensive for the businesses that hire them. While it is crucial to possess the needed experience and qualifications needed to become a consultant, a solid background in consulting is also required to become competitive in the advertising consulting market.

The definition is given by the U.S. Bureau of Labor Statistics (BLS) to the advertising consultant is a person who produces the procedures and ideas needed for marketing and advertising purposes. Once an advertising consultant is hired by a client, he or she is responsible for creating a suitable advertising campaign, starting with proving the creative solutions needed to elaborate the campaign ideas.

In the recent years, as more companies go through massive downsizings, career consultants are more in demand than ever.

The job of a career consultant is to provide advice and well-founded information about what career choice should its clients follow. A career consultant may also recommend certain training that an employee facing redeployment or redundancy requires in order to remain active in the today's job market.

The duties of a career consultant usually range from offering appropriate help; running workshops addressed to recently relieved personnel, client's personal characteristics assessment, helping with the problems a client's faces, devising action plans and counseling clients to offering assistance with job applications, resume renewal and other job seeking dealings. In other words, a career consultant is a person who will help you when you are in need of finding another job.

If you wish to start a career in career consulting it is best to possess a psychology degree or qualifications in career guidance or personal management. Of course, relevant experience is always a plus, as a few years of relevant work experience is always enough to determine a client choose you in spite of a new entry, which is only now gathering the experience needed in this domain. As a career consultant, you should also possess the following skills: excellent listening skills, beyond average verbal and written communication skills, confidence and a non-judgmental attitude.

INFORMATION TECHNOLOGY CONSULTING

As long as you have relevant know-how about software, hardware, and everything that stand in between, and you are willing to share that information with the customers, you will not have any problems in finding clients and making a career out of computer consultancy.

Computer consulting or IT consulting as it is also known is the field of consultancy that specializes in advising companies on how to use their resources better in the pursuance of achieving their business objectives.

IT consultants advise, plan, install and design the information technology mainframe needed for a business to successfully operate in the today's market. As an IT Consultant, you must possess both excellent technical skills and outstanding interpersonal skills, a potent combination that is very sought after in today's market.

As an entry-level IT consultant any relevant degree is acceptable, but as you further develop your career, a number of additional courses and qualifications might be required of you to be able to progress further. An expert IT consultant can possess qualifications in niche domains such as operational research, engineering, business studies or software engineering. But for graduates, it could be enough to possess a postgraduate IT conversion course.

A skilled IT consultant should possess good problem-solving skills, analytical skills, multi-tasking ability, a meticulous approach to work and a good time management.

EXECUTIVE SEARCH (HEAD HUNTER) CONSULTING

Companies might be caught in a downsizing trend today, but in spite of this trend, head-hunter Consultants (Executive Search Consultants) are in great demand, due to everlasting seek towards finding great personnel

An executive search consultant is in charge of the huge responsibility of finding suitable top position candidates to fill positions such as CEO and top management. Because finding the best-qualified executives for every job, companies usually ask the help of specialized consultants who possess great experience in dealing with this endeavor.

Because a typical company, which is seeking to hire a new upper executive, CEO or senior manager cannot use a classic recruitment agency, these companies can either choose to hire its executives by searching in-house or seek the help of specialized individuals who have made a career out of this effort. An executive headhunter must find the best alternative for the opened position, having in mind all the company's needs and strategic plan.

As an executive search consultants you will have the next responsibilities: to conduct the candidate interest according to the corporate plan, to listen to the client's needs carefully, to implement the actual search using your own database of candidates or other specialized tools, and actively search for new candidates by making use of every novel means available.

HUMAN RESOURCE CONSULTING

As long as people will have the right to think and work freely there will always be some personnel problem in every company. It is only normal. This means that there will always be the need for human resources consultants.

The human resources consultants are the people who are charged with the well-functioning interpersonal work dynamics that every company is seeking today. By being in charge of the personnel influx, training, and proper integration, a human resources consultant must actively seek to achieve the company's goals by ensuring the quality of the hired personnel.

Besides that, an HR consultant is usually called into action to advise the company with an entire array of issues that involve its hired workforce. An HR consultant can very well work on their own or associated with a larger HR Consulting company.

The typical HR consultant has the following responsibilities: to advise the management on to how to better manage the workforce, to prepare and deliver regular reports, to prepare and present the required training sessions, conduct audit over the HR activities, elaborate certain HR programs and services in the pursuance of creating the optimal work environment.

PUBLIC RELATIONS OR PR CONSULTING

As mentioned at the beginning of the book, good media coverage has the power to make a booming business out of every venture and of course, on the other side of the palm, bad media coverage can destroy every business, big or small.

To ensure that nothing but the best reaches the press, companies usually hire specialized consultants to help them with the public relationship affairs. A public relations consultant can have a wide array of roles, ranging from writing press releases to organizing events and public speaking.

In short, a public relations consultant is in charge of handling the public image of the hiring company, whatever that might mean. This makes this career the perfect option for those who are seeking novelty and want always to be on the move, never settling in the same kind of work every day. A typical public relations consultant may have the following roles, depending of course on the type of company he or she is representing: organizing events, writing regular articles regarding the activity of clients, keeping good media relations, developing good promotional strategies and so on.

Whether on your own or hired by a larger public relationship consulting company, you must always be performing at your best, since all your clients will depend on the kind of image you put into the market about them. Every failure in this job reflects poorly on the clients you are representing, so there will always be a great pressure involved into this kind of work.

MANAGEMENT CONSULTING

In this field of work, the experience is everything. If you wish to advise managers and executives on how to do their work better, you must really know your work. Management consultant help companies solve their most pressing matters, maximize income, create value and improve overall performance. In doing so, management consultants regularly operate at a level involving organizational structure, management, strategy, and operations; they are charged with finding the best options of approach and offer a recommendation on how a business can become more competitive on the market.

The typical responsibilities of a management consultant are highly complex and vary according to the client that hired them. Some of the usual tasks may include: collecting data and research, regular clients interview, creating business proposals, running workshops and focus groups and regular meeting with the shareholders.

Added to those responsibilities mentioned above, the typical management consultant might be charged with: identifying issues, generating solutions and presenting them to the clients, implementing recommendations, help executives in making relevant business decisions.

INSURANCE CONSULTING

Every company needs insurance, and the consultants who help them with choosing the best available option are professionals that make use of their statistical knowledge and mathematical skills in order to determine the client's financial risk and the best insurance policy that will fully cover it in the case of calamity.

The insurance consultant also generates long-term financial forecasts used by either the board of executives or by the government itself in taking well fundamental decisions, regarding the local market and its risks.

Besides those mentioned above, insurance consultants can also be charged with a wide range of additional services like risk management, pensions, corporate recovery or acquisitions. They are also the ones responsible with the actual pitching of options, in front of the deciding board, helping them choose the best option that will answer their company's needs.

As a standard, to be able to make a career in insurance consultancy, one must possess a bachelor's degree in a field like economics, business administration ordinance, but of course, most clients work for relevant work experience in every

nsultant they hire. This means that it will be a bit difficult to
et it all started in this domain of consulting.

But a good money management experience, great customer
service skills, great attention to details and good interpersonal
skills can favor you in getting those first contract needed to
build your portfolio.

EDUCATION CONSULTING

Almost half of the students today have no idea on what career
they should pursue once they finish their educational cycle. And
with the current employment market being as it is, there is no
wonder the demand for education consultants is rising fast.

An education consultant is a person in charge of optimizing the
student's potential in accordance with his or her inborn abilities
and potentials. In doing so, an education consultant brings
relevant information on relevant available school programs,
spends time with the client and tries to find the best
educational path together with him or her and provide a wide
array of academical testing to optimize the students' academic
potential and to follow up on the client's educational progress.

All of this in the pursuance of creating the best educational path
that the student (client) can follow, so by the end of the
educational cycle the client will be fully prepared to face to job
market on a very competitive level.

BUSINESS CONSULTING

Business consultants are specialists who are hired by
companies to do two main things: To detect problems and
generate the required solutions to fix those problems.

No matter what type of problem a company faces (management problems, sales decrease or issues with cash flow); they know it is best to ask help from a specialist instead of trying to fix the issue internally. Doing so has turned out to be more time and cost-effective than the alternative even it at first it might not seem this way. By doing the required testing and research, a business consultant can detect the cause of the problems much faster, and with a heightened precision then it would be possible by making use of other alternatives.

Of course, after the problem is identified and isolated, the consultant must offer the best solution for it. After detecting the problem that is dragging the company down, the consultant must sit at the same table with the executives of that company and discuss the best possible approach, needed to fix the issues. It is said that the initial cost generated by hiring a consultant might be high, but in the long run is highly worth it, since a problem left untreated tends to escalate into more costly versions of itself.

A business consultant usually comes from business backgrounds and possesses a great amount of field experience. To be a successful business consultant, it is said that one must be a successful business owner or executive.

BEAUTY & FASHION CONSULTING

Beauty and fashion consultants sell their expertise regarding beauty products that are best suitable for the hiring client. Because every individual is built differently from one another, beauty products don't work the same way for all of us. The efficiency of a product can depend on a lot of variables such as skin tone, complexity, sensitivity, hair density and even face construction.

All beauty and fashion consultants must have a welcoming and friendly personality, be able to communicate well and possess excellent customer skills, since the most of his or her daily activity will involve working with people, in stores or on the field.

This job doesn't require any particular qualification. Instead, you'll need a sharp appearance and high personal hygiene standards, completed with the right client-oriented attitude.

As part of this job, one might find himself or herself spending time with customers, giving customers samples of your products and helping them apply those products if need be, keep customer records and handle cash and specific products.

PERSONAL CONSULTING

Personal consultants are here to help people identify their goals, articulate their ambitions and advise realistic plans that will help them succeed in life. In addition to that,

A personal consultant might offer therapy sessions, life coaching, or in most cases both, all in the pursuance of creating positive change in the life of the client. The normal daily tasks of an personal consultant are to understand the client's needs, establish a lucrative relationship with the client, understand what makes the client tick better than the client itself, helping them arrange their priorities in the order of their importance, monitor the progress and step back when their work is done, leaving the client to live his or her life without further assistance.

The typical personal consultant has a background in psychology, but with enough relevant experience, this background requirement can be successfully bypassed.

If you should seek a career in personal consultancy, you should be willing to focus more on the client than you do on yourself. It might sound redundant, but believe me when I say that this is where most personal consultants fail.

ENVIRONMENTAL AND CONSERVATION CONSULTING

Environmental and conservations consultants are professionals who help companies in their pursuit to reduce their emissions. In doing so, those consultants play a huge role in reducing the overall industrial impact on the environment. By becoming an environmental and conservation consultant, one will be charged with the company's environment policy evaluation, an audit of the management systems and processes and measuring the overall exterior contamination that the hiring business produces.

In doing so, the environmental and conservation consultant helps the client with designing and implementing of more efficient processes and systems in the pursuance of future environmental impact reduction.

As an added bonus, you will be able to travel a lot since your activity will closely relate to field plants and overall field activity, and you will have the satisfaction that you contribute to the overall well-being of the planet.

SALES CONSULTING

Sales consultants are the bridge between a client and a company. They are the ones charged with building long-term relationships between the two, promoting the company's products and services and addressing the needs of the clients at hand. Sales consultants may work either for a company or on their own.

While the self-employed sales consults can set their own working schedule and level of income, being more independent, the ones hired by a sales consulting company benefit from regular bonuses, benefits, and a set salary.

The key responsibilities of a sales consultant are as follows: to identify and meet the needs of the customers, maintaining good business relationships, providing in-depth information about the products and services they are selling, keeping a journal of the client meetings and past successful sales.

Successful sales consultants work closely with their customers and clients throughout and after the sales process, ensuring that the needs of both sides of the deal are fully satisfied. Consultants identify the needs of the clients and try to address those needs by making use of the product or service he or she is selling. Besides those mentioned above, sales consultants might find themselves attending a sales meeting, handling client's objections and issues, processing orders, working with a wide array of corporate departments, scheduling appointments, meetings, and calls and sometimes even devise the sales strategy of the client company.

OFFLINE MARKETING CONSULTING

(Jim and I work in this field)

An offline marketing consultant is a highly skilled professional charged with implementing all marketing methods for a company, excluding, of course, the online marketing methods. Since this industry is as old as commerce itself, the market doesn't lack highly skilled marketing professionals that have made a career out of offering their help to others.

Over the years, the marketing dynamics have changed due to the advancement of technology, but at the core, those dynamics have remained almost the same, meaning that advertisement in magazines, newspapers, print media, billboards, busses and exhibition shows have remained at the core of offline marketing. In this field of work a consultant may advise his clients to do everything it can be done to reach their fans and customers, without making use of the online tools and methods; those are another part of marketing we will speak soon enough.

Offline marketing helps immensely in increasing revenue, brand awareness and popularity, maximizing profit, and overall local reach. The only difference between online and offline marketing is the medium within the marketing activities are deployed, the rest is just about the same, meaning that both marketing branches follow the same premises, being the reach of audiences by making use of all means available.

To become an offline marketing consultant, a suitable university degree might be required but enough, since marketing, indiscriminate of the medium in which it's applied, revolves around one single focal point, and that is an experience.

SOCIAL MEDIA CONSULTING

There are more than 10 million social media consultants worldwide. Just a single search on Google will return huge numbers, all having something to do with social media consulting.

The need for social media consultants has skyrocketed in recent years since more and more businesses, and public figures go online. This means that more and more entities are looking to promote themselves in a medium that nothing is forgotten, and everything is remembered and used against you even after years have passed. Because of this huge pressure, the majority of firms and public persons that have gotten online seek the help of social media consultants to be sure that everything that goes online is by the image they want to promote themselves.

Being a social media consultant means more than knowing how to set up a YouTube, Facebook or Twitter account. It means knowing the customer base, their needs and wants and that you have to create the content you send to them accordingly.

To become a social media consultant no degree or fields of study are required. But, on the other hand, it can help to have marketing or psychological or educational background, since you'll work with tens of thousands of people at once and the content you publish has the potential to reach millions.

BRANDING CONSULTING

When it comes to providing analysis, general marketing expertise and solutions regarding on how companies can successfully sell their products, branding consultants are the people you can ask for assistance. They usually work with management consulting firms and stand in close quarters with the company's clients and marketing executives. Besides that, branding managers work to develop and implement branding campaigns and strategies for existing products and new ones alike, depending on the current corporate expansion plan.

The duties of a branding consultant may include gathering data, targeting certain markets, performing market research, consumer perception assessment, internal audits, and overall goal reach assessment.

To become a branding consulting, a bachelor's degree in business or marketing may be required of you. Besides that, experience in a field such as sales, finance or communications is highly valued. If one should desire further career enhancement, he or she could opt for the completion of a marketing or business master's program. Besides all of that, relevant field experience is always valued by clients and companies in this field of work.

ONLINE MARKETING CONSULTING

As an online marketing consultant, one is charged with the handling of one or more companies' online advertising. The online marketing consultant's job is to increase sales, revenue and the amount of weekly traffic that is directed to one or more of the firm's active websites.

To be able to perform such strategies, a marketing consultant might work with elaborate online marketing plans, search engine optimization, e-mail campaigns and other specialized techniques meant to increase traffic and overall online visibility.

The typical responsibilities for an online marketing consultant range from the identification of new online marketing opportunities, evaluating existing market standards, optimizing the current company's branding, writing online content, managing cross-platform content and supervising email campaigns, to tracking and reviewing analytics regarding the overall marketing activity.

No field of study is required for an online marketing consultant, except a relevant bachelor's degree and usable work experience. Besides these, a heightened sense of attention to details and psychology studies might be good to have.

FOOD AND BEVERAGE CONSULTING

The final consultancy field in our top twenty lists is food and beverage. The food and beverage consultant's job is to provide advice for existing businesses such as restaurants, fast food, taverns, casual dining, hotel, resorts, hospitals, bakeries and so on.

Because of the strict compliance standards, intense competition, and low-profit margins, food, and beverage companies are forced to comply with the current standards of business.

The economy, however, is steadily improving, and the food and beverage industry is shifting towards a new millennial point of view that is highlighting the consumerism aspect of our behavior. In doing so, the food and beverage consultant must be able to create loyalty towards the hiring brand.

On top of that, a food and beverage consultant must be able to offer the best possible approach towards finding out the issues that keep the customers from earning more.

Five Questions to Ask Yourself Before You Start a Career in Consulting

If by now a career in consultancy seems like the best-suited job for you, you should start by answering the following questions:

AM I AN EXPERT IN ANY FIELD? ✓

Experts are not made overnight. To become a fully prepared field expert, you must invest at least a couple of years into a particular domain. Most consultants work for half their lives in a particular domain before they take the required steps towards becoming a consultant.

If you want to become a consultant, you should start by developing your skills in a particular domain and never stop until you reach an expert level. Otherwise, you may have trouble finding clients who are willing to listen to you. It is known that the biggest sellers in the field of the consultancy are experience and notoriety. Without those two it will be very hard to sustain a career as a consultant.

If, however, you possess a certain degree of expertise in the fields mentioned above or any other field for that matter, maybe it is time to undertake the steps towards building a career in consultancy. Continue by asking yourself the following questions:

AM I A PEOPLE PERSON? ✓

Expertise alone will not get you very far in this world. Maybe it's enough to secure a well-paid job, but as a consultant, you need to be able to understand and interact with people more than everyone.

If you are not very skilled at interacting with other people, don't worry, there are excellent courses on intrapersonal skills and social dynamics you can find online or offline. Such a website is www.geocosbur.com. There you can find all you need to know about how to interact with people and how to always make a good impression.

DO I HAVE GOOD COMMUNICATION SKILLS?

Being a people person means that you must possess good to great communication skills. In this field alone, it utmost important to know what to say, when to say it and how to say it. As a consultant, the image is everything, and that can be ruined as easy as one two three with a few improper words. If you think your communication skills may need to be polished up, there are hundreds of online courses, audio books and PDFs you can use to learn those highly required skills.

DO I TAKE REJECTION WELL?

A big drawback in the field of consultancy can be the way you handle rejections. And believe me when I say there will be a few. Clients won't start queuing at your doorstep right from the start. In the first one to three years, you'll need to call a lot of people and sell your services the hard way. This means that you will have to make hundreds of cold calls, send thousands of emails and deal with hundreds of rejections.

All you need to know is to stay focused and don't let rejections drawback on you. Instead, focus on your successes and keep on pushing. You'll get there soon enough.

Do I have what it takes to be successful?

George-Cosmin Burlacu, one of Romania's best personal development trainers, said that in order to become successful you must first <u>define your own version of success.</u> This means that you must clearly know what being successful means to you and keep that mental image always in your mind.

Once you have defined your own version of what it means to be successful you only need two more things: perseverance and determination.

As Robin Sharma says, all change is hard at first, messy in the middle and so gorgeous at the end. And you should know any path towards success starts with change.

Once you have addressed all the above questions, it is time to start working on your new career perspective:

Now let me give you a self-analysis. I never considered myself as an expert. Well, I was not an expert. Let's face it; working at a classified department of a newspaper doesn't make some an expert on anything.

I was never a people person so to speak. Even Jim knew this early on when we met. But I had somewhat decent communication skills, so that was something positive going for me.

I didn't take rejection too well. I always became defensive if and when someone criticized my work or even rejected my ideas.

But I knew I had this desire, this drive, that one day I want to go to the top, I want to be successful, and I was willing to do whatever it takes to get there.

Jim told me, even though I lacked 3 out of the five skills needed to be a consultant, he explained to me that the drive is to be successful can overcome the rest of the shortcomings.

Slowly but surely I started reading books about how to become a people person, how to grow self-confidence and started to understand what Jim was saying.

5 Pre-Start Steps You Should Take

Before starting, you'll need to test your products (service in our case). This means that you must offer your counsel to friends and close ones for free. Always ask for sincere feedback and ideas for improvements. Do this a couple of times and see how it goes.

The worst thing you can do is to quit your day job only to find out that your services are not good enough or have no demand on the market. Instead, try offering consultancy as a hobby at first. Quit your job only when you have enough clients to sustain all your financial needs.

A few other things you can do while you are "testing the waters, are to prepare some questionnaire for your prospective clients, the type of questionnaires that would give you an idea what and how they may need your help. Prepare a contract that you would have to offer your future clients in the event they want to hire you (A sample contract is attached at the end of this book). Make a spreadsheet of fees that you want to charge to your clients.

Try to make it at least 3 tier pricing, where the first tier would be for a minimum service; it is the "special" price for you to get you through the door. Next the second tier pricing would be the mid-level one, and finally, the third tier or the final tier pricing is where you include all the "bells and whistles." This is your full package deal and highest tier pricing, this for the clients that want everything. But make sure to explain what each tier includes and what it doesn't include, this way everyone can compare and see what level they are most comfortable with.

Here are the five pre-start steps you should take:

1. Soul Search

Your very first step is to soul search deep in your mind and see what type of consulting clicks with you, what type of work motivates you, get you excited. It will help if you have some basic idea about the subject too.

2. Zero in on the Best One

Say you come up with 2-3 ideas from all the soul-searching. It's time to analyze them and pick the best one. Write down all the positive and the negative of each idea and see which one carries more "positive" then pick that idea.

3. Read and Study the Subject

Now that you picked the best one out of all, time to get to work. Time to educate yourself on this topic. In this phase, you have to do a lot of reading and taking notes. Anything you read that sticks with you, write them down on a notepad for later use. Check on Amazon, see what are the best-selling books in your field, find at least 2-3 and read them A to Z.

4. Research the Trend of your Industry

Jim's recommendation on this is to do a Google search, find a few great blog sites, forums and trade magazines. Read and analyze them to learn what the new trends in your industry are.

5. Find and Meet Successful People in Your Industry On and Offline

Time for you to network, this will help you two ways. First, you get to learn from the experts and second, once you get to know them, you can even get work from them. Often some of the very successful consultants turn down jobs, but if they know you well, and know you can do a good job, they may send those "turn down" jobs your way. This is exactly what happened to me. Jim gave the mini-jobs when he didn't have time for them. That is how I got started.

It is easier to find them online than offline, so start with Facebook and do a search for Facebook groups that are relevant to your subject. You can then do the same with Twitter. One of the best places for a consultant is LinkedIn; this is one of the top professional networking site. So make sure you have a great profile page in all of them

Lastly, get some business cards and letterheads done. Make sure they look truly professional. Learn how to write and send professional proposals. It won't hurt to practice dressing up like a true professional. After all what other ways you can portray confidence other than dressing up in some nicely fitted suits.

How to Actually Get Started

Once you have determined that your services are welcomed or even demanded by the market, it is time to head right in and properly start your consulting career. No matter if your domain of expertise is a niche or not, you should start building a client base right away. The best way to start is by building a website. Your website is the best place where people can find relevant information about your work and how to get in contact with you.

Besides a website, you should also start a blog, and join a couple of relevant online discussions. It could be Facebook, Twitter, LinkedIn, forums or any other relevant places. Remember to always leave a link to your site so that people who are interested in your work can easily find you.

Your website should be professionally designed, and you should provide easy to understand the content. One important part is your "About Me" page, make sure to write a few paragraphs about who you are and why you are an expert in your subject and what makes you a great consultant in your market.

If you are looking to build a website or a blog, the best way to do it is by hiring a professional for a couple of hundred bucks from one of the online talent hiring places like upwork.com or freelancer.com. But make sure to have your domain and hosting account ready before you hire the designer.

The best place to buy a domain name, in my opinion, is from Name.com as they are the cheapest when it comes to renewal, unlike Go Daddy or few other domain registrars who would sell you a domain for 99 cents but next year it may cost you $30 to renew that same domain. I found out Name.com charges the same price for both which is around $9/year. Next step is to go to Bluehost.com and but a shared hosting account.

When buying a domain remember to pick a name that is catchy, creative and explains what it is all about, or you can just buy a domain that says your name, like if your name is John Doe, then look and see if johndoe.com or johndoe.net is available. This way your name is the brand you are trying to establish. If you want to search and see if your name is available to buy go HERE to search.

Here is a 5 step Checklist you can follow

- Build a Website/Blog
- Join a few professional networks on and Offline
- Create professional looking business cards and letterheads
- Get active in online social media
- Find professional conferences in your industry and join

How to Land the Clients

Building a website and creating online awareness is a great way to start your client base, but if you want to expand that client base and reach even more relevant people, you should go where your clients are. This means that you should go to networking events, gatherings and conferences. Also, this is the time when you need to pick up the phone and start making some calls.

Steps to get your first client:

1. Identify the issues in your industry that your future clients are facing.

Let's face it, in every industry, there is a pain, and there are issues. First, you need to find those pain points, those issues.

2. Identify the clients who may need your help

Next, find out which companies are the likely sufferers from these pains and issues.

3. Contact them, meet them explain the "pain."

Contact them, ask to meet them, and chances are if you contact 20 companies, you may get to meet only 7 of them, but that is okay. Once you meet, explain the "Pain," the Issues the market/industry is facing and why you think you are the best one to solve it.

4. Offer them a solution to solve the "Pain."

Last, offer them a solution which should be a simple process, offer your service but be very clear and transparent.

Consulting Procedures

Depending on your area of expertise, the consulting procedure might vary accordingly. Be that as it may, all consulting procedures have several things in common. You should build your consulting procedure from scratch, based on the need to identify the client's problems or issues correctly and to offer the best solutions to address your client's problems and issues.

As we mentioned in Pre Start-Up Steps, it is best to have a plan before you meet your first client. Have questionnaires ready, have a clear understanding once you are hired what and how you want to approach your work. Be confident but have a plan. It is better to gather up as much data as you possibly can before actually consulting your client on the topic.

If you are hired to work for a company where there are employees, we often ask permission first to speak to the employees and ask their opinion on how and what they think the solution to the problem is. Once you get their answers, write them down and analyze each and every one and come up the negatives and positives for each answer, then go back the employees that gave the best answers and run the negative sides of their answers (from your analysis) and see what their replies are.

Next, you can start summarizing some of the best answers to the problem you are working on and put them on paper along with your own analysis and ideas. Once you are confident that these are the best solution to their problem, have a meeting with the people that hired you, run those solutions by them and get their feedback. Based on the feedback, decide if you need to go back to the drawing board or should you help them implement some of that solution and see the results.

How to Market Yourself

When it comes to marketing yourself, you should start with Social media, networking and then move to local area marketing. My advice is to seek assistance from specialists in your field, as long as you are not a marketing consultant yourself, then you'll probably know what to do.

If for some reasons, you cannot afford or don't want to seek help with your marketing, you can always invest more in your Facebook page where you can upload meaningful content, start a Twitter account with regular updates and news and upload short educational videos on your YouTube account.

On Twitter, you can always do a search for a specific keyword. Say your niche is personal consulting. If you search for the word "personal consulting" you will likely find a few hundred to maybe a thousand people who have an interest in that subject. Once you have that list of people, start to follow them, and you will see few of them will follow you back in return. This way you are slowly creating a network.

But to grow your Twitter followers, you do have to post useful and valuable links and content to share and share someone else's content that you think is valuable (retweet).

This is the very strategy you can follow and implement in most other social media sites like Facebook and LinkedIn too.

This will do wonders for your overall online visibility. Just don't forget to link your social media accounts and your site together.

You can even hire a social media marketing expert from one of those freelance sites. A hired expert can help you set up your profile in all various social media platforms; they can also help you link to various relevant sites, find you people and sites to follow and set up links as well.

Here is a list of sites where you can hire people to do your website, to help you market yourself.

upwork.com

Guru.com

Freelancer.com

How Much to Charge

The price of your services should always be fair. Always try to provide more value than you are paid for and do some research on what other consultants from your field of work are charging.

A first start small, at about 75% of the price of your completion, this will make your services attractive from the financial point of view and will also tell your customers that you know what you are doing since you don't sell yourself too cheap.

As your brand expands and you gain more and more experience, you may want to increase the price of your service to 100% of the price of your competition and even higher.

But first, you need to find out how much your competitors are charging. For this, you need to do some extensive research. Again use social media to do this research. Try to find some other experts/consultants in your field, pose as a client and ask them how much they charge for their service.

Set your price accordingly, but make sure to check at least 3-4 competitors before setting up your own price.

How to Grow Big

To be successful in this field of work, you must never stop learning. People seek your expertise and advice because you know more than they do. This means that you must always be at the forefront of every new information and technology in your field.

As the demand for your consulting services grows, you may want to consider hiring other people to handle the auxiliary activities such as selling, marketing and so on. Also, as you expand even further, you may want to hire consultants that can take care of some of your workloads.

Often you will see once you get started with your first consulting job, the 2nd one will come more easily than the first one. Similarly, the 3rd, the 4th and so on will come with greater ease. It is your work, your network and the reference that will land you clients after clients.

It is always a great idea to start networking with companies in your field by finding out all of their social media presence and actively corresponding with them, become their friends, go to seminars where your future clients may go. Introduce yourself, drop them your business cards, mention names of other companies that you worked with before.

Make sure to complement some of their great work achievements and tell them how much you admire their company and that you would be honored to be a part of their team. Everyone loves flattery; it can get you far sometimes, but do not overdo it.

The last word, make sure to do plenty of research on these companies beforehand, so when you meet some of them in seminars or wherever, you can talk intelligently, and they would know that you know about their company and their achievements.

Last Words

In conclusion, I can say that the field of consulting is a noble career path with many satisfactions and a fair amount of obstacles. If you possess the right expertise, excellent people skills and take pleasure in helping other people reach the same level of success as yourself, maybe this field of work is the right choice for you.

Just remember most successful consultants have three character strengths, CONFIDENCE, KNOWLEDGE and COMMUNICATION SKILL. Practice all three of them, and you will see success!

Good Luck!

Sample Consulting Contract

ABC Corp.

CONSULTING AGREEMENT

This Consulting Agreement (this "Agreement") is made as of
_____, by and between [Company
Name], a Delaware corporation (the "Company"), and
_____ ("Consultant").

Consulting Relationship. During the term of this Agreement,
Consultant will provide consulting services to the Company as
described in Exhibit A hereto (the "Services"). Consultant
represents that Consultant is duly licensed (as applicable) and
has the qualifications, the experience and the ability to properly
perform the Services. Consultant shall use Consultant's best
efforts to perform the Services such that the results are
satisfactory to the Company. Consultant shall devote [at least]
[_____% of Consultant's time/_____ hours per week] to
performance of the Services.

Fees. As consideration for the Services to be provided by
Consultant and other obligations, the Company shall pay to
Consultant the amounts specified in Exhibit B hereto at the
times specified therein.

Expenses. Consultant shall not be authorized to incur on behalf
of the Company any expenses and will be responsible for all
expenses incurred while performing the Services [except as
expressly specified in Exhibit C hereto] unless otherwise agreed
to by the Company's [Title of Officer], which consent shall be
evidenced in writing for any expenses in excess of
$_____. As a condition to receipt of reimbursement,
Consultant shall be required to submit to the Company

reasonable evidence that the amount involved was both reasonable and necessary to the Services provided under this Agreement.

Term and Termination. Consultant shall serve as a consultant to the Company for a period commencing on _____ and terminating on the earlier of (a) the date Consultant completes the provision of the Services to the Company under this Agreement, or (b) the date Consultant shall have been paid the maximum amount of consulting fees as provided in Exhibit B hereto.

Notwithstanding the above, either party may terminate this Agreement at any time upon _____ business days' written the notice. In the event of such termination, Consultant shall be paid for any portion of the Services that have been performed before the termination.

Should either party default in the performance of this Agreement or materially breach any of its obligations under this Agreement, including but not limited to Consultant's obligations under the Confidential Information and Invention Assignment Agreement between the Company and Consultant referenced below, the non-breaching party may terminate this Agreement immediately if the breaching party fails to cure the breach within _____ business days after having received written notice by the non-breaching party of the breach or default.

Independent Contractor. Consultant's relationship with the Company will be that of an independent contractor and not that of an employee.

The method of Provision of Services. Consultant shall be solely responsible for determining the method, details, and means of performing the Services. The consultant may, at Consultant's own expense, employ or engage the services of such employees, subcontractors, partners or agents, as Consultant deems necessary to perform the Services (collectively, the "Assistants"). The Assistants are not and shall not be employees of the Company, and Consultant shall be wholly responsible for the professional performance of the Services by the Assistants such that the results are satisfactory to the Company. Consultant shall expressly advise the Assistants of the terms of this Agreement and shall require each Assistant to execute and deliver to the Company a Confidential Information and Invention Assignment Agreement substantially in the form attached to this Agreement as Exhibit D hereto (the "Confidentiality Agreement").

No Authority to Bind Company. Consultant acknowledges and agrees that Consultant and its Assistants have no authority to enter into contracts that bind the Company or create obligations on the part of the Company without the prior written authorization of the Company.

No Benefits. Consultant acknowledges and agrees that Consultant and its Assistants shall not be eligible for any Company employee benefits and, to the extent Consultant otherwise would be eligible for any Company employee benefits but for the express terms of this Agreement, Consultant (on behalf of itself and its employees) hereby expressly declines to participate in such Company employee benefits.

Withholding; Indemnification. Consultant shall have full responsibility for applicable withholding taxes for all compensation paid to Consultant or its Assistants under this Agreement, and for compliance with all applicable labor and employment requirements with respect to Consultant's self-employment, sole proprietorship or other form of business organization, and with respect to the Assistants, including state worker's compensation insurance coverage requirements and any U.S. immigration visa requirements. Consultant agrees to indemnify, defend and hold the Company harmless from any liability for, or assessment of, any claims or penalties with respect to such withholding taxes, labor or employment requirements, including any liability for, or assessment of, withholding taxes imposed on the Company by the relevant taxing authorities with respect to any compensation paid to Consultant or its Assistants.

Supervision of Consultant's Services. All of the services to be performed by Consultant, including but not limited to the Services, will be as agreed between Consultant and the Company's [Supervisor's Title]. The consultant will be required to report to the [Supervisor's Title] concerning the Services performed under this Agreement. The nature and frequency of these reports will be left to the discretion of the [Supervisor's Title].

Consulting or Other Services for Competitors. Consultant represents and warrants that Consultant does not presently perform or intend to perform, during the term of the Agreement, consulting or other services for, or engage in or intend to engage in an employment relationship with, companies whose businesses or proposed businesses in any way involve products or services which would be competitive with the Company's products or services, or those products or services proposed or in development by the Company during the term of the Agreement (except for those companies, if any, listed on Exhibit E hereto). If, however, Consultant decides to do so, Consultant agrees that, in advance of accepting such work, Consultant will promptly notify the Company in writing, specifying the organization with which Consultant proposes to consult, provide services, or become employed by and to provide information sufficient to allow the Company to determine if such work would conflict with the terms of this Agreement, including the terms of the Confidentiality Agreement, the interests of the Company or further services which the Company might request of Consultant. If the Company determines that such work conflicts with the terms of this Agreement, the Company reserves the right to terminate this Agreement immediately. In no event shall any of the Services be performed for the Company at the facilities of a third party or using the resources of a third party.

Confidential Information and Invention Assignment Agreement. Consultant shall sign, or has signed, a Confidential Information and Invention Assignment Agreement in the form set forth as Exhibit D hereto, on or before the date Consultant begins providing the Services.

Conflicts with this Agreement. Consultant represents and warrants that neither Consultant nor any of the Assistants is under any pre-existing obligation in conflict or in any way inconsistent with the provisions of this Agreement. Consultant represents and warrants that Consultant's performance of all the terms of this Agreement will not breach any agreement to keep in confidence proprietary information acquired by Consultant in confidence or in trust prior to the commencement of this Agreement. Consultant warrants that Consultant has the right to disclose and/or or use all ideas, processes, techniques and other information, if any, which Consultant has gained from third parties, and which Consultant discloses to the Company or uses in the course of the performance of this Agreement, without liability to such third parties. Notwithstanding the foregoing, Consultant agrees that Consultant shall not bundle with or incorporate into any deliveries provided to the Company herewith any third party products, ideas, processes, or other techniques, without the express, written prior approval of the Company. Consultant represents and warrants that Consultant has not granted and will not grant any rights or licenses to any intellectual property or technology that would conflict with Consultant's obligations under this Agreement. The consultant will not knowingly infringe upon any copyright, patent, trade secret or another property right of any former client, employer or third party in the performance of the Services.

<u>Miscellaneous</u>.

<u>Governing Law</u>. The validity, interpretation, construction and performance of this Agreement, and all acts and transactions pursuant hereto and the rights and obligations of the parties hereto shall be governed, construed and interpreted in accordance with the laws of the state of California, without giving effect to principles of conflicts of law.

<u>Entire Agreement</u>. This Agreement sets forth the entire agreement and understanding of the parties relating to the subject matter herein and supersedes all prior or contemporaneous discussions, understandings and agreements, whether oral or written, between them, relating to the subject matter hereof.

<u>Amendments and Waivers</u>. No modification of or amendment to this Agreement, nor any waiver of any rights under this Agreement, shall be effective unless in writing signed by the parties to this Agreement. No delay or failure to require performance of any provision of this Agreement shall constitute a waiver of that provision as to that or any other instance.

<u>Successors and Assigns</u>. Except as otherwise provided in this Agreement, this Agreement, and the rights and obligations of the parties hereunder, will be binding upon and inure to the benefit of their respective successors, assigns, heirs, executors, administrators and legal representatives. The Company may assign any of its rights and obligations under this Agreement. No other party to this Agreement may assign, whether voluntarily or by operation of law, any of its rights and obligations under this Agreement, except with the prior written consent of the Company.

Notices. Any notice, demand or request required or permitted to be given under this Agreement shall be in writing and shall be deemed sufficient when delivered personally or by overnight courier or sent by email, or 48 hours after being deposited in the U.S. mail as certified or registered mail with postage prepaid, addressed to the party to be notified at such party's address as set forth on the signature page, as subsequently modified by written notice, or if no address is specified on the signature page, at the most recent address set forth in the Company's books and records.

Severability. If one or more provisions of this Agreement are held to be unenforceable under applicable law, the parties agree to renegotiate such provision in good faith. In the event that the parties cannot reach a mutually agreeable and enforceable replacement for such provision, then (i) such provision shall be excluded from this Agreement, (ii) the balance of the Agreement shall be interpreted as if such provision were so excluded and (iii) the balance of the Agreement shall be enforceable in accordance with its terms.

Construction. This Agreement is the result of negotiations between and has been reviewed by each of the parties hereto and their respective counsel, if any; accordingly, this Agreement shall be deemed to be the product of all of the parties hereto, and no ambiguity shall be construed in favor of or against any one of the parties hereto.

Counterparts. This Agreement may be executed in any number of counterparts, each of which when so executed and delivered shall be deemed an original, and all of which together shall constitute one and the same agreement. Execution of a facsimile copy will have the same force and effect as execution of an original, and a facsimile signature will be deemed an original and valid signature.

<u>Electronic Delivery</u>. The Company may, in its sole discretion, decide to deliver any documents related to this Agreement or any notices required by applicable law or the Company's Certificate of Incorporation or Bylaws by email or any other electronic means. Consultant hereby consents to (i) conduct business electronically (ii) receive such documents and notices by such electronic delivery and (iii) sign documents electronically and agrees to participate through an on-line or electronic system established and maintained by the Company or a third party designated by the Company.

The parties have executed this Agreement as of the date first written above.

The Company:

ABC Corp.

By: _____

      (Signature)

Name: _____

Title: _____

Address:

_____

_____ _____

United States

CONSULTANT

_____

      (Print Name)

_____

      (Signature)

Address:

_____

Email:_____

Helpful Resources

Definition of Expert

http://www.businessdictionary.com/definition/expert.html

DOMAIN AND WEBSITE HOSTING

Name.com for Cheapest Domains

Bluehost.com For hosting your website or blog

HIRE EDITOR, DESIGNER, LOGO DESIGNER, SOCIAL MEDIA EXPERTS FROM ONLINE

Freelancer.com

Upwork.com

Fiverr.com

Made in the USA
Las Vegas, NV
12 September 2021

30141141R00036